High, Flat, Down And Back Up Again!

INSIGHTS ON BIPOLARITY
Challenges and hopes

Alain Amzallag, Ph.D. (ABD)

authorHOUSE®

AuthorHouse™ LLC
1663 Liberty Drive
Bloomington, IN 47403
www.authorhouse.com
Phone: 1-800-839-8640

Published by AuthorHouse 06/24/2014

ISBN: 978-1-4208-2502-2 (sc)
ISBN: 978-1-4634-7360-0 (e)

Library of Congress Control Number: 2005901373

This book is dedicated to my Mother:
Mrs. Eliane Amzallag, Z''L
Rosh Hodesh Nissan, 5764

March 22nd, 2004

NOTE FROM A FRIEND

Dear Alain,

I had the opportunity to read your book and I must say that I found it very emotional but also uplifting to read.

Your summary reflects what a strong person you are and it also demonstrates how critically important faith is in one's life.

I believe your writing has also given me insight into my sibling's thought patterns as well; who as you know also suffers from a mental disorder.

I have great respect for you as a person due to your perseverance and determination to make a contribution and share your experience with others.

Clearly your determination and character has come through in your children who are well-rounded, creative and charitable.

You have done a wonderful job showing your appreciation for those that have given you strong support through your life.

I have been enriched by knowing you as a friend and co-worker and your book will educate friends and family of those with Bipolarity (M.D.I.) as well as those diagnosed with it.

God Bless you and your family as you continue to search for and find the beauty in the world.

Roxane-October, 2004

FOREWORD

Foreword to the book *High, Flat, Down. And Back up Again. A Guide to Manic-Depressive Illness.*

More than 4% of the population suffers from a bipolar disorder with mood swings from highs to severe depressions. The most severe form, Bipolar 1, is also known as manic-depression (M.D.I.) in which the highs of manic episodes are much more intense.

In the past, this illness was less understood and surrounded by many taboos and much prejudice. Fortunately in the last few years the understanding and treatment of this illness have greatly improved and many of the taboos have fallen thanks to the courageous work of many people who had publicly identifyed themselves as being manic-depressive or bipolar. In this book, Alain Amzallag continues in this tradition, and tells his story from the inside with warmth and humor. You will find both an informative and an inspiring tale full of hope for today and the future.

Much of world history has been influenced by bipolar people who had the courage and energy to change the world around them. After you read this book, join your local bipolar association and help to improve the understanding and the acceptance of this remarkable illness in your community.

After all, there are not many illnesses that can actually help people be even more successful in their life!

This Foreword was written by Brian Bexton, M.D., FRCPC – President of the Québec Psychiatric Association and Vice-president of REVIVRE (Anxiety, Depression and Bipolar).

TABLE OF CONTENTS

PART II:
MY JOURNEY

OVERVIEW

BIPOLARITY: Scourge or Blessing?

In this guide to Manic-Depressive Illness (Bipolarity) I will attempt to illustrate some of the positive and some of the negative aspects of this condition that will enable you to decide for yourself whether the advantages conferred by Bipolarity outweigh the disadvantages or whether in fact, the opposite is true. I am still debating this issue myself as it has been difficult to be objective. By necessity, the contents of this guide are somewhat autobiographical in nature in order for the reader to understand the background events that preceded my first manic episode, the events surrounding that fateful first episode and everything that followed.

The most important event of my life was the onset of my mother's cancer as this event, combined with the mood swings and the psychological and emotional precariousness inherent in individuals affected by M.D.I., propelled me into an eleven year journey of turmoil and despair sprinkled with hope. Praying and asking rabbis as well as ministers of other faiths for blessings of good health for my mother were full time endeavors. These blessings were probably helpful to my mother and certainly to me.

This guide is intended for readers interested in the various aspects of M.D.I. and will be best appreciated by those who took their science courses seriously in high school. I apologize if I occasionally got carried away with scientific terminology, but at times I have been unable to find a simple and accurate way to express a word or an idea.

I have written this guide with two goals in mind. The first is to help at least one person affected with Bipolarity go through his or her life with an increased understanding of what is happening to him or her. The second is to enlighten the general population as to the joys and tribulations engendered by M.D.I. and to contribute to the awareness of the plight of psychiatric patients in general. The support of family and friends is essential to individuals affected by mental illness and donations and support for research and treatments are important.

CHAPTER I

AFFECTIVE DISORDERS:

BIPOLAR AND DEPRESSION

In <u>Mental Illness: A regional handbook for families</u>[1] there is a meaningful and informative paragraph on Affective Disorders which I am transcribing below for the reader's benefit:

Affective disorders or mood disorders include depression and bipolar affective disorder (manic-depressive illness). These are common psychiatric problems and affect five percent of the adult population at any given time. The essential characteristic is a disturbance in mood. Bipolar or manic-depressive illness is characterized by cycles of depression and/or mania. Manic symptoms may include the following: boundless energy, enthusiasm, and need for activity; rapid loud disorganized speech; short temper and argumentativeness; involvement in activities which have painful consequences such as shopping sprees, reckless driving, and unwise business investments; delusional thinking. When depressed the person may have difficulty sleeping; lose interest in daily activities; lose his appetite; suffer feelings of worthlessness, guilt or hopelessness; exhibit feelings of sadness; be unable to concentrate; experience extreme irritability.

Major depression (described above) should not be confused with reactive depression or the "Blues". Reactive depression, sometimes called Situational Affective Disorder, is a temporary condition triggered by life problems. Should this condition persist, the affected person should consult a doctor to find out if it is becoming a major depression.

---

[1] Mental Illness: A regional handbook for families was developed in 1992 by Ami-Québec Alliance for the Mentally Ill Inc. and Agency for Reintegration in the Community (Project ARC Inc.) and the 4th edition appeared in 2003.

CHAPTER II
MEDICATIONS

Individuals affected by bipolarity must actively participate in their treatment by giving feedback to their medical professional about any side effects they may experience and how they are feeling. This two-way interaction between the psychiatrist and the patient can lead to a relatively stable and non-chaotic life.

It is my experience that persons with Bipolarity should never miss a dose of medication. However, if an individual falls asleep without taking his or her bedtime meds, he or she should not double the next dose.

My experience with medications for Bipolarity is limited; however, I will do my best to offer the reader a brief overview. The general categories I will cover are: mood stabilizers, anti-depressants, and neuroleptics.

Mood Stabilizers: (Tegretol, Epival, Lamictal, Lithium Carbonate, etc.)

Lithium Carbonate (Carbolith, Lithane, and Duralith) is a mood stabilizer. As you know, people with Bipolarity can be "high" or "down". What lithium does is reduce how intense a "high" the patient experiences as well as diminish the depth of the "down" state. People on Lithium have to take this medication continuously and maintain a certain level of $LiCO_3$ in their blood at all times. Together with their psychiatrist, who will prescribe the test, your medical professional will determine the level of Litium Carbonate in your blood and the frequency of testing required in order to monitor your levels over time.

Under the heading of Mood Stabilizers, this is a presentation based on an article by Isabelle Artus and sections summarized by Didier Chos, on how nutritional elements can help regulate variations in mood.

Dopamine, Serotonin and Noradrenalin are neurotransmitters that jointly regulate mood, energy level, harmony and indeed determine our "Happiness". When the level of serotonin is insufficient, the mood dips rapidly, sometimes leading to aggressive behavior; this is followed by sleep disorders, bad mood and sometimes depression. Serotonin is labeled the "Good Humour Hormone". A precursor to both serotonin and dopamine is the amino acid Tryptophan and seeking foods that contain Tryptophan is necessary to maintain a stable level of these two neurotransmitters. Starchy foods, fish, rice etc. contain Tryptophan. However, too much simple sugars, and/or stimulants like nicotine or caffeine reduce the serotonin content in the brain. This happens because your system depletes your serotonin reserve a while after you ingest these substances. You ingest these substances; you get a high and your mood crashes a few hours later; thus the addiction cycle continues.

REMINDER: balanced blood sugars levels promote balanced mood. To achieve a balanced mood, you need enough serotonin producing protein and insulin balancing polyunsaturated"good"fats.

Now, "a deficiency in dopamine leads to difficulties in concentrating and to a loss in motivation, Dopamine is geared to stimulate the heart and general metabolism. Noradrenalin increases motivation and energy levels and acts as an anti depressant as well". "A non-essential amino acid L-Tyrosine found in seafood, cheese, milk and eggs, is a precursor to noradrenalin and dopamine, adequate energy level and a good dose of optimism, the aforementioned foodstuff should be eaten".

Warning: It is of paramount importance for the reader to realize that the aforementioned nutritional tips cannot replace prescribed medications, but they can enhance their efficacy.

Many medications have side effects and, having had my share of trials and errors, I can affirm that with almost every medication, the side effects are temporary, the body and the brain get used to them and they become irrelevant. However, long-term usage of lithium can cause irreversible damage to the thyroid gland, the kidneys and other organs. This is why regular monitoring of Lithium levels is essential. This ensures that the optimal amount of lithium salt is delivered to the body in order to perform the intended beneficial effects, while minimizing the destructive potential of the drug.

Anti-Depressants :*(Prozac, Paxil, Effexor, etc.)* some new-generation anti-depressants include: Manerix, Remeron and Welbutrin.

I struggled for many years with the fangs of depression, which usually hit me in October and November. I found that Light Therapy helped to some extent but recently Effexor proved to be the right medication for me.

Neuroleptics: Moditen, Largactil, Orap, Zyprexa.

Neuroleptics slow down the electrochemical impulses between neurons at the synaptic level. The neuroleptic I am currently taking is Orap (2mg). I have been using it for over 25 years and it has served me well. With my psychiatrist's authorization, I have used Orap as a dampening tool for hypomania. As soon as I feel euphoria, manifested by an increased appreciation of beauty in nature, objects, music, art, I immediately increase the dose of Orap to 3, 4 mg depending on the need. The upper limit, never to be crossed, is 10 mg Orap/day. In this fashion, I was able to avoid psychiatric hospitalization from 1981 to 2002 – an incredible and remarkable achievement for anyone who suffers from Bipolarity, type 1. I am grateful to my ex-wife Emma who helped tremendously by providing me with a mirror and monitored my hypomanic elevation and directing me to increase or decrease the amount of Orap.

This pre-authorized technique of adjusting the neuroleptic dose requires constant and lifelong observation of one's mood, one's state of euphoria and one's general state of mental health. This technique is extremely difficult to master, especially during the period of neuroleptic adjustment. It is even more difficult to do without a partner or a parent who can act as a mirror because you are being asked to evaluate the effect of a neuroleptic medication. In the meantime, you are using the brain cells that are being affected by the very neuroleptic medication, the very effect of which you are being asked to evaluate. How can you be, at the same time, critical and objective? But with a mirror, it is possible!

I recommend to individuals with Bipolarity to wear a Medic Alert Bracelet (or Medallion) inscribed with their medical condition. The reverse charges telephone number on the bracelet can then be used to direct paramedics, law officials, and medical personnel to your medical information in case of emergency. The Boy Scouts say "Always Be Prepared" and the Medic Alert can come in handy if you are found in the street in a disoriented manic state, and can effect a speedy and efficient hospitalization during which the appropriate medical treatment can be administered.

It is very important to continue taking your medication until the end of the period prescribed by your psychiatrist. Especially in the case of treatment for mania or the alleviation of Manic-Depression, PLEASE DO NOT REDUCE THE DOSE OR THE LENGTH OF TREATMENT WITHOUT YOUR PHYSICIAN'S AUTHORIZATION.

The only exception is if you and your psychiatrist agree upon a plan that gives you the pre-authorization to modulate the medications under specific circumstances.

WARNING: After taking the medications for a while, you may feel, or appear to feel, better and the symptoms of mania and/ or depression may diminish or disappear. Nevertheless, you must continue taking them until you and your physician decide otherwise.

Your maintenance drugs, such as mood stabilizers and neuroleptics must become part of your everyday routine, a conditioned reflex taking them must become part of your everyday routine, a conditioned reflex action to take your pills upon waking up and going to bed. <u>Alcohol consumption can</u> be harmful because it decreases the efficacy of the medication and should be discussed with a health professional.

Also, is important to mention that these medications have side effects, sometimes beginning before the onset of the desired beneficial and therapeutic effects. Unless you are experiencing terribly uncomfortable and painful side effects (at which point you should contact your psychiatrist) try to tough it out since in most cases side effects are transient and benign. In general, do not stop medication without your doctor's authorization.

In general, do not stop medication without your doctor's authorization. If you go a full cycle without taking your medications, do NOT double the dose, just take your medications normally. The next cycle, your body will adjust to the missing dose but: DO NOT DO THIS VERY OFTEN.

> *"It's difficult. I take a low dose of lithium nightly. I take an antidepressant for my darkness because prayer isn't enough. My therapist hears confession twice a month, my shrink delivers the host, and I can stand in the woods and see the world spark."*—David Lovelace,

CHAPTER III
BIPOLARITY FROM WITHIN

Just imagine a bright morning in late March; you are taking a walk and everything appears crisp, fresh and clear. So clear, that you see the buds at the very tip of top branches; so fresh that you smell the symphony of perfumes from flowers and aromatic plants and so crisp that you hear every note of bird songs. In fact, every one of your five senses, or your perception of your environment through these five senses, is being stimulated to a heightened degree. It is a relief as now you are able to enjoy creation in all its magnificence after the sad, dark and somber months of winter.

The senses of smell and of taste combined lead individuals suffering from hypomania to have a proclivity for tasty foods and fine cuisine, which can be expensive to acquire and frequently lead to weight gain. Then, the other senses "kick in": the compelling desire to buy beautiful things such as items associated with music, art, literature, automotive products, etc. This state represents a relatively early stage of hypomania.

The next stage is an increased level of activity and this industriousness probably reflects the previously subdued desire to accomplish a concrete, important and significant achievement which in some cases would be intended to help "Society and/or Humanity".

Another characteristic of hypomania, and for that matter mania, is the disruption of the Biological Clock. Sleep patterns are disturbed to the extent that individuals with Bipolarity sleep very little at the hypomania stage and practically not at all at the manic stage. Midway through the climb to hypomania, individuals may undertake several ambitious projects that they cannot handle realistically.

Characteristic at that stage is also the effect on the quality, speed and delivery of speech which becomes rapid and to some degree slurred. The end of each word is gnawed by the beginning of the next one. I refer to this phenomenon as the "folding telescope effect", and this is the cue for me to seek serious help.

There is an inherent added difficulty with people like myself who take Lithium because Lithium Carbonate is a salt; a perpetual thirst has to be quenched, leading to frequent urination. During daytime it is a side effect Lithium takers learn to live with, however, during sleeping hours it is quite an ordeal. I get up 5-6 times a night to urinate and replenish fluids. It may help to know that reducing all stimulants such as caffeine, sugar and nicotine 8 hours before bedtime decreases thirst and curbs the need to urinate with such frequency.

I know I have very little talent for painting. I have applied my Bipolarity caused hypomania induced creativity (see front cover art) to produce 25-30 paintings. My style is "Mystical-flyé" and I have been told that in some very small ways it resembles Van Gogh's. It is interesting to note that Van Gogh had Bipolarity. As you will read later on, I am a very heavy smoker, but when I paint (always in a hypomanic state) I am overtaken by an exhilarating feeling of well being, of elation and internal joy. This inner contentment is so intense that I forget to smoke for up to 6-7 hours compared to my usual consumption of one cigarette every 22 minutes. Expression, whether verbal, artistic or musical, engenders liberation of the most precious, delicate, beautiful and harmonious components of the inner self of a slightly hypomanic bipolar person. These feelings make somewhat credible my contention that Bipolarity (M.D.I.) is almost worth having.

Irritability can set in either during hypomania or major depression. When irritable, annoying and bothering things are amplified and I am impatient with people, even those behaving according to normal criteria. I have a tendency to "snap" at close relatives as they are the ones who love me and whom I love, and hence represent "safe targets".

When I am antagonized, I yell and usually dismiss myself by leaving the premises in a stormy fashion after a heated argument.

These periods of irritability, in my case, last from three days to two weeks, and with a frequency of two to three times per year.

Full fledged mania is accompanied by a total loss of control, mostly of what comprises reality. Perception of the world, reality and surroundings during a manic episode, is greatly affected by the individual's state since they usually have interrupted taking their medication at that stage. Some medical researchers invoke that a chemical is missing in the brain and that this is why this phenomenon occurs. With full-blown mania, usually I am transported by ambulance to the Emergency Room, medically assisted and processed and I land in the psychiatric ward where I am pumped up with tranquilizers in order to restore normalcy and non-pathologic reality. Then, I sleep a very long time and upon wakening I have, of course, my first cigarette. The thing I most clearly recall on the psychiatric ward is the six cigarettes per day limit, to be compared to sixty to seventy per day on the outside. This constraint causes tremendous cravings and has, in my opinion, very few beneficial effects.

Following a manic episode, there is a recovery period (see chapter on Rehabilitation) during which relatively quiescent times enable me to return to complete normalcy. Also, during this period of recovery, I make resolutions which will enable me to better detect and be better prepared to recognize the precursor signs of hypomania and mania.

Often at this stage, a state of major depression begins. It has been stated that 20% of the general population will at one point in their life suffer from mental issues. However, depression in people with Affective Bipolar Disorder is several orders of magnitude more intense, severe and painful then regular depression. The sensation and feelings accompanying major depression are difficult to describe. Let me just say that you wish to "Get out of your body"; figuratively and sometimes literally. You wish you were back in your mother's womb or that your spirit and soul leave your body to join the heavens. The later alternative is anathema to me due to my religious beliefs, my faith and intense love for life; love that is only sporadically permitted to be expressed due to recurring conditions of hypomania, mania, irritability, major depression and hospitalizations

Anyone considering suicide should perhaps view this suffering as a <u>TEMPORARY ORDEAL</u> that you have simply have to go through. You only have to hold on for just a little while longer... and <u>SEEK HELP IMMEDIATELY!</u> Suicide Hot Lines, Hospital Emergency Rooms, Police and Fire Stations are accessible to help and assist you. At that stage, YOU NEED HELP!

"There is a particular kind of pain, elation, loneliness, and terror involved in this kind of madness. When you're high it's tremendous. The ideas and feelings are fast and frequent like shooting stars, and you follow them until you find better and brighter ones. Shyness goes, the rights words and gestures are suddenly there, the power to captivate others a felt certainty. There are interests found in uninteresting people. Sensuality is pervasive and the desire to seduce and be seduced irresistible. Feelings of ease, intensity, power, well-being, financial omnipotence, and euphoria pervade one's marrow. But, somewhere, this changes. The fast ideas are far too fast, and there are far too many; overwhelming confusion replaces clarity. Memory goes. Humor and absorption on friends' faces are replaced by fear and concern. Everything previously moving with the grain is now against—you are irritable angry, frightened, uncontrollable, and enmeshed totally in the blackest caves of the mind. You never knew those caves were there. It will never end, for madness carves its own reality." Kay Redfield Jamison, *An Unquiet Mind: A Memoir of Moods and Madness.*

CHAPTER IV
REHABILITATION

Recently, I came to realize what I was attempting to achieve during my rehabilitation. Actually, it was my young cousin, Valérie M. who helped clarify my objectives. She stated that what I was striving for was to take the following decision: And this was to make a Voluntary Vow of Simplicity in my life. This vow entails a reduction in income, devoting time to find out who I am, to take care of and improve myself, to do constructive things that are rewarding to me and others, to people who have needs to be fuelled or suffering to be alleviated, to commune with Nature and with the Magnificent Creation of the Lord. And above all stay away from the rat race and make do with less material things.

Whether after the onset of mania or deep depression leading to attempted suicide, hospitalization is required.

After hospitalization, the Day Hospital is an option for psychiatric patients. Group therapy, Occupational therapy, individual sessions with psychiatric nurses, psychologists and psychiatrists help create a life plan for recovering patients. Social workers can help the patient with financial and/or housing matters. This is a big recovery step!

St. Mary's Hospital stated goal of the Rehabilitation Service: "The Rehabilitation Service aims to improve participants' quality of life and assists in integration and adaptation to community living. It provides individual sessions and group activities designed to help participants cope with life stresses as they develop self care, social, leisure, education and work skills"

Rehabilitation Services at St. Mary's presently offer:

A) Transition from Psychiatric Ward

B) Stress Management Workshop

C) Self Esteem Workshop

D) Relaxation techniques

E) Exercises

F) Clerical Workshop

G) Craft & Therapeutic Activities

H) Young Adult Recovery Group

I) Dialectical Behavior Group

J) Individual Occupational Therapy.

It has been my experience that rehab health professionals treat you with dignity, care and respect. They help you define your needs, find some answers and coping mechanisms, and facilitate your integration in the community. Personally, I have achieved most of my rehabilitation oriented goals with hard work and outstanding leadership during workshops from a psychiatric nurse, Michelle de Gonzague and spectacular individual occupational therapy with Katarina Kovacevich. I have made a lot of progress but I have some ways to go still.

What follows are eight "tips", inspired by "The Consumer's Guide to Recovery from A to Z" by Geanette Keil which I now try to keep them, an integral part of my "Modus Vivendi":

1- It is important to take time to be alone, to hear yourself think, to have pleasant thoughts, to surround yourself with beautiful images, sounds and items and to learn to appreciate the sounds of silence. You might also want to indulge in the music of Chopin, Mozart, Beethoven, Tchaikovsky, and so on. Elevation and fulfillment of the soul as well as tranquility and serenity will be attained.

2- Whether you believe in Life, G-d or a Creative Entity, what matters is that your beliefs lead you to spiritual considerations, feelings and thoughts. Believing that out there or all around us there is a causative factor at the origin of the Universe and hence of the World, your World and your Life, leads to some spiritual peace and comfort which results in a tremendous reduction in stress caused by metaphysical and Bipolarity related anguish and anxiety.

3- Whatever and whenever you must decide between two or more alternatives, it is a good idea to reflect briefly before taking action ponders for a few seconds before taking action. A wise way to proceed before making choices is to ask yourself the following question: Is the choice I am making Good and Healthy for Me in my Life?

4- SLEEP is a tremendous healer for the body, the nervous system and (most importantly for persons with Bipolarity) for brain function. Individuals should listen to their body and sleep as much as required I also recommend naps during the day provided they do not interfere with work or scheduled activities.

5- Behave with moral values in activities and work. If you do not, negative feedback might ensue and the extreme sensitivity of persons with Bipolarity may cause emotional unpleasantness and even stress or pain. Acting proactively for the good gives you a sense of self worth and satisfactions you make the right choice of words and/or actions.

6- Excess in any direction is not advisable Individuals affected with Bipolarity are prone to ups and downs. During the rehabilitation process, and afterward strive to follow the middle road. This is extremely difficult for people with Bipolarity but, remember that any improvement is a victory for you. Following the middle road will generate more stability and equilibrium in your life.

7- Nutrition has to be regarded as a prime element in mental health. Nourishment to your body and your brain affects the way you feel physically and mentally. The brain utilizes simple sugars in order to function. This simple sugar is present in a wide variety of foods, in the form of complex carbohydrates when digested. A balanced diet with regular meal times supplemented two or three snacks, will ensure a constant supply of simple sugars to the brain and will preclude the occurrence of hypoglycemia (low blood sugar). Components of certain foodstuffs help synthesize neurotransmitters that send messages to the brain. Three of them help regulate mood: dopamine (trigger), NorEpinephrin (enhancer) and Serotonin (slows things down). Our neurochemical harmony depends on the balance between these three chemical substances. This is why it is important for individuals with Bipolarity to inquire about which foods to eat at what period of the year in order to have a handle on mood stability (see mood stabilizers section in Medications Chapter).

8- Determine what your unique talents are, develop them to the hilt, express yourself through your talents and in the process you'll instill joy in your life of others. This is true generosity.

"Knowing yourself is the beginning of all wisdom."—Aristotle.

CHAPTER V

RELATIONSHIPS

WITH MENTAL HEALTH PROFESSIONALS

Your lifeline to sanity is your psychiatrist. He or she is a highly trained medical professional who can also draw upon experiences and insights gained with other psychiatric patients. He or she has life experience <u>TRUST HIM or HER</u> However, excessive familiarity, personality conflicts and in some instances, breaches of professional conduct can all become obstacles to a positive relationship with your doctor.

Psychiatrists are authorized to prescribe medication. You must help the doctor by being truthful and rigorously precise in your feedback about the effect of your meds and also about whatever problems are currently causing you a lot of external and internal stress. Through honest discussion with the psychiatrist he/she will be better able to use the tools of medication and psychotherapy.

The Psychologist is not a medically trained Mental Health Professional. He or she will listen to you, help you to unravel the knots of unresolved incidents or situations and generally help you understand why you do or do not do certain things. The psychologist works in conjunction with a psychiatrist in order to prescribe appropriate medication.

During hospitalization in a psychiatric ward, the patient benefits from the skills of a number of health professionals: psychiatrists, psychologists, psychiatric nurses, occupational therapists, music therapists and social workers. Very diligently, professionally and with rigor intermixed with kindness, they unite their efforts to restore the patient's health.

Sometimes following hospitalization, the psychiatric patient is directed to a Day Hospital where he or she is semi-autonomous. After the Day Hospital period, the patient is assigned a Psychiatrist in the Out-Patient Clinic. It is of paramount importance for the individual suffering from a mental disorder to keep consulting the psychiatrist as often as the patient and the doctor feel it is necessary.

Keep your appointments and arrive 15 minutes before the time of the appointment in order to quieten and reflect on your issues and progress (Lombardi time).

Many mental Health professionals may seem cold, harsh or overly restrictive. In fact, I think this is a protective shield they have acquired in order to remain sane and objective as they are continually bombarded with emotional problems and verbal outbursts from numerous patients. Try not to take it personally.

"Minds that have withered into psychosis are far more terrifying than any character of fiction."—Christian Baloga.

CHAPTER VI

LIGHT, LUMINOSITY AND BIPOLARITY

It is undeniable that light, the quantity, intensity and duration plays an important role in the emotional state of everyone. When the weather is overcast, we're not as chipper as when the sun is out bright and shiny. It is believed that light interacts with a very small gland deep in the brain, the pineal, which, when stimulated by light, releases hormones into the body, similar to endorphins.

In the spring, the individual with Bipolarity who is exposed to increased daylight and luminosity feels much better, so much better that it may lead to hypomania and potentially to mania. It seems to me that the individual with Bipolarity is slow in adapting to the increase of light, causing an overproduction of the pineal hormone that can start problems and this causes an overproduction of the pineal gland hormone with the aforementioned consequences.

Taking this further, individuals with Bipolarity generally have a difficult time adjusting to jetlag. Travelling across time zones lengthens or shortens the period of daylight. For me, I have chosen not to travel by air from east or west since 1982. I believe it was a good decision, as I have had only one manic episode since.

The corollary of the spring phenomenon is the Fall-Winter decrease in daylight as the days grow shorter. Those who do not suffer from mental illness may experience the 'Blues', but for individuals with Bipolarity, the decrease in daylight can trigger a major depressive episode. In Scandinavia and other countries of the Upper Northern Hemisphere, supplementary artificial light (fluorescent or incandescent) has been successfully used to treat depression during winter.

In my own experience, seeking well lit places in Montreal as well as travelling North-South to Florida or Mexico for a 10 day vacation has helped reduce depressive states in winter. The difference in the Latitude of these locations provides more daylight, sunshine and luminosity–all desired benefits to a depressed person.

Please note that some medications such as Lithium, Melatonin, Tetracycline, St.John's-Wort, Phenothiazines, Hemat- oporphyrins, acne creams, and creams with Retinoic Acid, Cloroquine and other Chemotherapy Drugs can make you very sensitive to light. – Northern Light Technologies – www.northernlighttechnologies.com

CHAPTER VII
THE GENETICS OF BIPOLARITY

As a preamble to discussing the hereditary aspects of Bipolarity, please allow me to review one pertinent law of heredity: Mendel's first law of dominance and recessiveness. Some simple genetic systems function as follows.

Say one gene has two forms and that when two genes of the same form are present (one obtained from the father and one from the mother), the characteristic dictated by that identical pair of genes is expressed. Take the gene for eye colour as an example. If the person inherits two genes for brown eyes, the brown colour will be expressed and the person will have brown eyes. Similarly, if the person inherits two genes for blue eyes, the blue colour will be expressed and the person will have blue eyes.

Now, what happens if one parent contributes a gene for brown eyes and the other parent contributes a gene for blue eyes? You probably know the answer already: the child will have brown eyes. This is because the brown gene for eye colour is dominant over the blue eyed gene which is therefore said to be recessive.

This law of dominance/recessiveness is pertinent to Bipolarity because a lot of evidence points to the recessive nature of the Bipolarity gene(s). Familial studies indicate very clearly a pattern of inheritance for Bipolarity, type 1. In addition, there is molecular genetic evidence for the presence of several genes (on different chromosomes) involved in the expression of Bipolarity.

In very simple terms, I have two doses of the gene because I am afflicted with Bipolarity, both my parents are carriers of the gene (i.e. they have a non-Bipolarity gene and one gene for Bipolarity at that location on a specific chromosome). They don't have expressed Bipolarity because it is necessary to have two genes for Bipolarity at that location; one each originating from both their parents, for Bipolarity to be manifested. I believe both my parents are carriers and that I had around 25% probability of getting from them both, at once, their chromosomes with the Bipolarity gene(s).

A number of years ago, I read a scientific article which stated that the gene for Bipolarity was linked (i.e. co-inherited) to other genes in very close proximity on that chromosome. Among them is a gene leading to above average creativity and intelligence as well as a gene which makes it extremely difficult to sever an addiction to tobacco, drugs and/or alcohol. This complex of genes (complex loci) represents as far as we know what persons with Bipolarity had transmitted to them from their parents as regards Bipolarity and determines, in part, the initial emotional and psychological state (predisposition) that will eventually, (with a severe environmental trigger) develop into a few manic and major depressive episodes, followed by the ups and downs (mood swings, hypomania and irritability) characteristic of the illness.

The ever quickening advances of science made possible by the success of the Human Genome Project will also soon let us see the essences of mental disease. Only after we understand them at the genetic level can we rationally seek out appropriate therapies for such illnesses as schizophrenia and bipolar disease. James D. Watson – *Nobel Prize laureate.*

With the advent of the Human Genome Project, it is possible nowadays to sequence completely, and in a few days, the genes that comprise an individual's genetic makeup. This opens the door to "Gene Therapy". In early 2014, in an In-Vitro Fertilization experiment in mice, scientists were able to create an offspring without an undesirable gene. It is noteworthy that men and mice have 97% of their genetic material with an identical sequence. In a few years, it will be possible to achieve gene therapy with humans and in the process create designer babies and individuals. However, for gene therapy in humans to be beneficial to humanity, it must be accompanied by the most stringent ethical restrictions so as to preclude the resurgence of the ugly head of Eugenics. Alain Amzallag, Ph.D. (ABD)

CHAPTER VIII

STIGMAS & TABOOS

STIGMAS AND TABOOS

Stigmas are the negative thoughts and attitudes that the general population manifests toward mental illnesses. People are sometimes condescending, fearful and unfair (particularly within the job market) to individuals who suffer from mental illness mainly due to ignorance and lack of information about these diseases.

Individuals affected with mental illnesses need, are entitled to, and deserve support from not only their loved ones, but also from the general population. Snide remarks, sneers and tasteless jokes are definitely counterproductive to the healing process and often leave the sufferer with a deeper feeling of rejection and alienation.

Learning about and understanding the origins and cause of the phenomena associated with these illnesses will result in the abating and the erosion of these detrimental stigmas and taboos.

Taboos:

The friends and families of a mentally ill person often experience a sense of helplessness, shame and fear because of the stigmas associated with these illnesses, because of their own lack of knowledge and because of the worrisome fear that they themselves may one day be affected. As a result of these factors, the friends and loved ones of a mentally ill person tend to be secretive, going to great lengths to hide the illness from others. This often results in a lack of the support that is desperately needed by their loved one. In their shame, they will shield themselves and their loved one from groups and from gossip that are perceived as detrimental. Also, family and friends often withdraw from the affected individual out of their fear and misunderstanding of the uncharacteristic, emotional outbursts that can accompany these diseases.

"STIGMAS AND TABOOS FEED ON EACH OTHER, CREATING A "CATCH 22" SITUATION (VICIOUS CIRCLE). IF ONE ATTEMPTS TO DISSIPATE AND REDUCE THESE TWO TANDEM PHENOMENA, THEIR IMPACT ON THE MENTALLY ILL AND THEIR FAMILIES CAN BE LESSENED."

We believe it is time that we start to put these stigmas and taboos behind us. We must realize that everyone has something in his or her lives to deal with, that everyone is "disabled" in some sense of the word. We believe that people, especially those suffering from mental illnesses, should become aware of their strengths and their positive attributes and focus on these. If family and friends support this process, recovery for the mentally ill person may be less fraught with difficulty. When people are afraid to open up, they miss the opportunity for support in all its ways and yet another vicious circle gains momentum.

It is ironic that anyone should associate stigmas with mental illness at all since the mode of hereditary transmission is not yet completely understood. This means that anyone is susceptible to becoming mentally ill! Indeed, epidemiological and statistical studies have shown that around twenty percent of the population, at some point in their lifetime, will suffer from some form of mental disorder. It is true that anyone who has had a relative who has suffered from mental illness is "at risk" for developing some forms of the condition themselves. Yet, just how much risk is impossible to determine or predict. We do know that genes are involved with these illnesses. It may be important to note here that ancestors, while they may have suffered from mental illness, were often undiagnosed and just labeled "eccentric".

Many individuals identified as mentally ill have conveyed to others, in writing, the story of their journey within and through a mental illness to a place of functionality. These individuals have written about managing their condition in order to become, or remain, operational. In addition to being a form of therapy, writing from our own perspectives and perceptions can very often be cathartic, allowing healing to take place. These authors encourage this process, as it benefits not only the writer, but may also benefit others making or watching such a journey. If you seek to publish it, who knows how many your story may inspire!

Families who are in the midst of the hurt and turmoil caused, in large part, by the silent aspect of the taboo should seek to obtain information from the many organizations who offer information and support; the Canadian Mental Health Association, the Mood Disorders Society/ Association of Canada, and a number of other organizations within North America. These organizations have been established to inform, support and also to create awareness and understanding of mental illnesses.

A person suffering from a mood disorder should not be subject to judgment or condemnation by any other member of society, including those closest to them. Rather, they need people to talk to and to support them during this time of deep personal crisis.

As knowledge and understanding erode these stigmas, it is our hope and belief that taboos will slowly release their stifling stranglehold, permitting the normalization and acceptance between an "affected family" and the "world outside".

LET US ALL PRAY FOR HUMANENESS TOWARD THE MENTAL WORLD

Alain Amzallag
Montréal, Canada

E-mail : alainamzallag@bell.net
 Web Site : www.alainamzallag.com

PART II:

MY JOURNEY

CHAPTER IX

MY FIRST 21 YEARS (1949-1970)

I was born in Casablanca, Morocco during the lovely month of May and was raised in a very loving, traditional Jewish family with three children. We lived in a villa that had a huge garden with all kinds of fruit trees, vegetation, lawns and a garage full of wooden and metal objects which, with the addition of a few tools, represented paradise for a young boy. The first sixteen years of my life were very happy. My parents imposed no chores; all I had to do was to concentrate on my studies and play.

My elementary school report card, when I was eight years old, states: "Intelligent student but emotional". These two words capture my essence and my predisposition for Bipolarity. They are opposite sides of the same coin and I believe these facets of my personality come from my inherited predisposition for Bipolarity.

Until I was sixteen, I interacted with Jewish, French, Spanish and Muslim people, and in the process, developed several close and enduring friendships. In 1962, I joined a scouting movement called Les Éclaireurs Israélites du Maroc and, except for an interruption from 1974 to 1990, I have been involved in scouting ever since. Scouting has been a positive and inspirational way of life for me.

In Primary School, I displayed an ability to do extremely rapid mathematical calculations in my head that led me to skip a grade. I entered The Ibn Toumert College when I was nine years old. During a Natural Science course in my first year of High School, I was drawn to and fascinated by the structure and function of the human body, memorized, drew and identified all the bones of the human skeleton and the names of most of the ligaments, tendon and nerves as well as the renal and liver functions.

With the exception of that Natural Science course, I was completely lost. At nine years old, I was simply too young to follow the regimen of a dozen or so different subject courses and, as a result, I was required to repeat the first year of High School.

Things stabilized at Lycée Lyautey, where I performed scholastically at an average to good level.

One major influence on my life happened at my Bar Mitzvah when my late great aunt Alice offered me a book entitled: Le Monde: Où va-t-il – d'où vient-t-il?, a collection of discoveries in several scientific and medical fields, making inquiries about the future and underlining the immensity of knowledge yet to acquire. At thirteen years old, I knew I had to become a scientist!

The following year (1963), my mother told me her brother Jacques died when he was forty years old. He was a cigarette smoker and died of throat cancer – may he rest in peace. This was when I subconsciously decided to focus my future scientific career in the direction of Cancer Research. This was the beginning of a subdued, unexpressed and underlying obsession to find a cure for cancer. This goal guided my future choices of universities, degrees, programmes, coursework, research and other learning opportunities. I sought the best possible preparation for the task of "curing" or finding better ways to treat this modern era "leprosy" referred to as cancer.

In 1965, my whole family immigrated to Montréal and I switched from a completely French High School system to Grade 11 in the English system. I did relatively well and was admitted to a four-year Bachelor of Science Programme at McGill University. The first year I studied very hard and obtained an 83% average. The second year, still interested in preparing myself for Cancer Research, I enrolled in the Honours Microbiology and Immunology Programme. The Microbiology dimension of the programme included both Bacteriology and Virology. I was particularly interested in studying viruses because they are implicated in the onset and/or transmission of certain cancers.

The Immunology coursework provided me with an understanding of the elements and mechanisms of immunity, which is relevant to the body's fight against Cancer (Immune Surveillance). During my first three years at McGill, I also enrolled in a variety of Chemistry courses because some chemicals are cancer-inducing through somatic and germ line mutations.

In the third year of my science programme, I switched Honours Programme to enroll in Bacterial Genetics. Again, Genetics plays an important role in cancer. The study of Genetics, its Laws, and its various mechanisms of gene transmission was essential to my preparation for Cancer Research. From July 1969 to August 1970, I worked on a research project in Bacterial Genetics with Jacky M. Somers (Post-doc) and Dr. Richard B. Middleton (Advisor). Together with them, my work was published in the <u>Journal of Bacteriology</u> in 1973.[2]

In my fourth year, I switched again to Honours this time, in Molecular Genetics. In parallel, I also took all of the courses in the Honours Biochemistry Programme. Although I felt to some extent inept, as well as scientifically and academically lacking, I had managed to acquire a tremendous amount of knowledge and scholastic ability, through very hard work and study combined with the gifts that Bipolarity had given me, retrospectively. In my own way, I had become a "Scientific Sherman Tank" pointed at the "Evils of Cancer".

"The only true wisdom is in knowing you know nothing."
—Socrates.

---

[2] Genetic Fine Structure of the Leucine Operon of Escherichia coli K-12. J.M. SOMERS, A. AMZALLAG, AND R.B. MIDDLETON. JOURNAL OF BACTERIOLOGY, Mar, 1973, p. 1268-1272

CHAPTER X
ADDICTION (1969-2013+)

Those who suffer from Bipolarity are very susceptible to strong addictions, mainly to drugs and alcohol.

In my family, and in my Sephardic Moroccan culture and tradition, we do not consume very much alcohol or use any drugs. In my parents' home and years later in my own family with my Emma, we used pure, natural grape juice on the Sabbath (instead of wine) for the weekly blessings. Probably, as a result of this, neither my siblings nor my children ever developed a taste or a need for alcohol.

When I was 18 years old, I rebelled by drinking Screwdrivers, Tom Collins, Rum and Cokes and Singapore Slings. A couple of years later, I realized how much I enjoyed them; I knew I could become an alcoholic very easily and so I stopped all alcohol consumption immediately. From the age of 40 until now, I have about half a glass of draft beer twice a year. Since my body isn't used to alcohol, it reacts swiftly and I become inebriated in a matter of seconds and I do NOT DRIVE FOR ANOTHER 5 HOURS.

However, as far as nicotine addiction is concerned, it is a totally different story!

From age 13 to 20, I was into physical activities up to 18 hours of different sports a week. In Dr. R.B. Middleton's laboratory, there was a married woman who smoked like a chimney. I became infatuated with her and in the process disobeyed one of the Ten Commandments. She offered me cigarettes. Within two weeks, I was hooked. This was by far the worst decision I ever made in my life.

Cigarette smoking has affected me terribly in so many ways, from the very basic to the very sophisticated, and has had a tremendous impact on my finances. I have calculated that in the 45 years that I have been a smoker, I have spent (capital + 10% compounded annual interest) the sum of $489,000 CND and counting. The house that I do not own went up in the smoke of my cigarettes.

There is no point in harping on the negative sides of smoking since smokers know about all the medical hazards, the smell that lingers on mouth, hands and clothes, etc. I would just like to mention that if I am still smoking, it is not for lack of trying to quit cold turkey, gradually or with good and valid methods. For a number of years, I have tried every new technique that has been developed – Nicoban, Nicorette, laser therapy, acupuncture, electroshock, hypnotherapy, Habitrol, Nicoderm, Lifesign Computer and several other available techniques – to no avail. Next time, I'll make sure not to covet someone else's wife!

For the last five years, I have given up trying to quit smoking as I have come to the conclusion that it is beyond my abilities. In order to protect myself from the potential development of cancer in my lungs, throat, palate, tongue and lips, I take a cocktail of the following detoxifying vitamins and minerals every morning:

Vitamin E – (400 international units per day) is believed to help repair lung damage caused by cigarette smoke (only weekdays).

Vitamin B12 – (500 mcg on the weekdays and 250 mcg on the weekends) to replace vitamin B12 depleted by nicotine.

Vitamin D – (3000 international units per day) has been shown to prevent cancer development in rats–Calcium Lab, McGill university-Royal Victoria Hospital.

Calcium – (500 mg per day) Antioxidant: meaning it neutralizes the oxidized state of DNA caused by mutations which could potentially lead to cancer.

Magnesium – (250 mg per day) Antioxidant – same as above.

Vitamin C – (500 –1000 mg per day during the winter) – Although the jury is not yet out on Linus Pauling's conclusions and assertions, vitamin C could be an antioxidant as well as a defense against the common cold.

I hope, and to a small extent believe that the reparative effects of these vitamins and mineral supplements will provide me with a certain level of protection against the carcinogenic chemicals in tar that constantly bombard my body

Other gifts that cigarettes have given me include bad breath, yellow teeth and fingers, chronic bronchitis (perhaps eventually leading to emphysema), burnt clothing, and the inability to embark on flights of more than 45 minutes for want of a cigarette. During movies, I have to leave the theatre 2-3 times to smoke. As a result of my nicotine addiction, I have been unable to attend classical music concerts, theatre, ballet, and opera for many years. It's pure hell! On the exceptional side, "Speed" was the only movie I saw in its entirety after getting up four or five times, going to the exit with my eyes riveted to the action on the screen and then running back to my seat.

If you are thinking starting to smoke, this warning: once you start, you've opened the door. From that point on, any increase of stress in your life will double, triple or quadruple your cigarette consumption. I believe that my inability to quit smoking cigarettes, despite numerous attempts, is related to my Manic-Depressive condition. Moreover, I believe that I could just as easily become strongly addicted to alcohol as a consequence of the expression of the Bipolarity gene (s).

A pitiful incident related to cigarette smoking occurred in 1987 while I was flying back to Montréal from a visit to the Canadian branch of Life Technologies INC in Ontario. I was hypomanic then and I requested a seat from Toronto to Montreal on a smoking flight – at that time, customers had a choice between smoking and non-smoking flights. However, the airline made a mistake and registered me for a non-smoking flight.

As I got on the plane, I heard the pilot on the P.A. system announcing the non-smoking nature of the flight. I was immediately hit by a panic attack, and attempted to get off the plane as I could not foresee staying almost two hours without smoking – something I had never done before. I was stopped by the steward. My speech was rapid and slurred, symptoms of hypomania; as I attempted to explain the situation. The crew thought I was a terrorist!! The pilot came out and said, "We have two choices: either you don't smoke and we fly to Montréal or we taxi back to the gate and check and search every piece of luggage". To which I replied, "You're giving me a hell of a choice". The flight was delayed by forty-five minutes while we argued. Finally, I relented and slept for most of the duration of the two-hour flight to Montréal. At one point, the steward offered me a cigarette, which I refused.

Once we arrived in Montréal, I gratefully smoked a cigarette in the terminal then I went back into the plane to speak with the steward. I told him that the reason I did not accept the cigarette he offered me while the plane was flying was that, although I don't always agree with it, I always obey the law, to which he replied, "I am glad you said that!"

"Clear your energy, honour your rhythm, live your vision." - George Denslow; *Living Out of Darkness: Personal Journey of Embracing the Bipolar Opportunity.*

CHAPTER XI

MUSIC (1966-2014+)

Unlike starting to smoke cigarettes, which is the most deleterious thing that I have ever done, volunteer work in Music Therapy in Geriatric Hospitals and Seniors' Homes is the most rewarding and gratifying endeavour I have undertaken in my life.

I learned how to play tunes on the recorder around campfires when I joined the scouting movement in 1962. My patrol leader Fortunato Chocron took the time and made the effort to show me the working of this simple instrument that produces such haunting sounds. As time went by, I learned to play more and more songs on it.

Because the first fourteen years of my life were those of a healthy young outdoorsman, no one suspected I might have some talent for music. I took piano lessons for three years and studied music scores on my own for an additional 40 years. I can now play at least 30 pieces on the recorder and 50 piano pieces.

My beginnings with Music Therapy date back to 1966 during my first year at McGill University. I played music for psychiatric patients at the Douglas Hospital with Andy Silagy, a classmate, (now Dr. Andrew Silagy, M.D.). I played the recorder and Andy accompanied me on his classical guitar. We were occasionally successful at helping patients express themselves. Our harmony and enthusiasm Andy and I generated reached the deep recesses of their mind at least for a time and sometimes unblocked them, at least for a time. Another time we were playing "Black Orpheus", a beautiful haunting Brazilian love song. At the end of the song a female psychiatric patient (in her fourties) who had not spoken for quite a long time, stood up, came towards me, kissed me on the cheek and said: "Alain, you're my boyfriend. I was only 17; I freaked out!

In 1995, when my late uncle Albert was in a Seniors' Geriatric Hospital. I visited him regularly and entertained him with some of his favourite music. I noticed that other patients in wheelchairs came closer and gathered around us, some clapping hands, some singing along and some just listening. This was the beginning of a great idea. I now entertain at a number of geriatric hospitals as a volunteer.

I am fluent in French and English, to the extent that when I am reading, writing or speaking in one of the two languages I am not always conscious as to which one I am using. This helped me assist my father in translating from English to French. Then, for several years I translated marketing and technical brochures from English to French at Canadian Life Technologies Inc. Sometimes, I switch involuntarily and unknowingly from English to French and back when I speak with a bilingual person. I also speak some Spanish, Modern Hebrew and Judeo-Arabic. My personal claim to fame is that during my pre-marriage days I learned and still know how to say "I love you" in over 31 languages. Might come in handy now that I am a free divorced man!

Although I have no scientific proof, I think and feel that the musical ability, the linguistic talent that has allowed me to pick up a few words in over 55 languages; my deep appreciation of Harmony in Art, Music, Ballet and Opera; my tendency to be deeply moved and softened by emotional moments and situations; my thirst for friendship, love, and human brotherhood, even if only at the community or neighbourhood level, are all connected to my Bipolarity in some way.

Even though Bipolarity can be terribly exacting during periods of extreme highs and of lows, I believe that all the gifts that I have been blessed with are meant to be developed to their fullest potential in the hope that I can use them to help my fellow beings.

When I started my journey as a Music Therapy volunteer in geriatric hospitals in 1995, I didn't know what was in store. There were groups of 25 to 40 residents, a piano, my recorder and I. I gave "concerts" intermixed with chatting (apparently my voice has soothing properties) and interacting with residents. They were interesting, wise, some forgetful (Alzheimer) and others who had suffered strokes. Some had musical talent from their earlier lives. Sometimes, if I played a tune they knew or related to, a beautiful and powerful tenor or contralto voice might rise above the melody and everyone would listen attentively to this unexpected talent.

At first, my experiences as Music Volunteer were very difficult for me, particularly when residents with strokes clapped with one hand on their wheelchairs to show appreciation of my music. Other conditions made me very sad and I would go home to my Emma and cry my heart out. But one gets used to everything in life, albeit gradually. One thing is certain, I provided the residents with harmony and enthusiasm and I lifted their spirits for a little while. I can honestly say that Music Therapy volunteer work in geriatric environments has become the most rewarding and gratifying endeavour I have undertaken.

In Numerology, it is said that a person's name predetermines some of his characteristics. Alain, my first name, means harmony in ancient Greek. Those who carry this name presumably seek and generate harmony. The 50 or so pieces I play on the piano are neither elaborate nor of high technical caliber but they are harmonious and I put all my emotions into the interpretations. I have always disliked dissonant music, much preferring Baroque, Classical and Romantic Era music as well as Jazz, Soul, Gospel – all of which have beautiful harmonic components.

"Music is a total constant. That's why we have such a strong visceral connection to it, you know? Because a song can take you back instantly to a moment, or a place, or even a person. No matter what has changed in your world, that one song says the same, just like that moment." – Sarah Dessen, *Just listen.*

CHAPTER XII

N.Y.C.—LEADING TO MY FIRST ATTACK OF MANIA (1970-1974)

In my fourth year at McGill University, I inquired about a good place to do Cancer Research in North America. Dr. Barid Mukherjee, Ph.D., Professor of Genetics at McGill University, and a good and kind man, pointed me to the Sloan-Kettering Institute for Cancer Research in New York City. Unbeknownst to me, Sloan- Kettering was in 1970 and probably is still considered the very best Institute in the World for Cancer Research. I applied and was readily accepted. Little did I know that the Ph.D. Programme at Sloan- Kettering was administered by the Cornell University Graduate School of Medical Sciences? This was an added bonus, as Cornell is an Ivy League school of high caliber. There are also several other great institutions involved in scientific and clinical research in the same area of East Side Manhattan (Sloan-Kettering Institute, Memorial Hospital, Cornell University Medical College, New York Hospital and Rockefeller University). Although I was eager to start laboratory work upon my arrival in N.Y.C. in September 1970, Cornell University insisted that all graduate students take one full year of courses. I quickly realized that my undergraduate training at McGill University was so intense and thorough that I could, to some extent, afford to skip some of the classes in order to attend the numerous lectures, seminars (sometimes hospital rounds) and presentations on cancer and other medical topics at any of the five institutions mentioned above. I was in scientific and medical research bliss.

Until the summer of 1973, everything went smoothly. My research, my academic studies and my social life were all going well. In June of that year, I met a woman of rare beauty. I fell madly in love with her and we had a relationship which was very intense and very erotic. Unfortunately, this was smack in the middle of the Free Love Era and after a few months, she was openly unfaithful to me. The tremendous emotional pain led me to expressions of anger. For the first time in my life, I became verbally abusive. The pain I felt was horrific, due in part to my excessive emotional vulnerability (latent Bipolarity) but also a result of my Jewish Moroccan upbringing which requires exclusivity between men and women who are romantically involved.

As a means of coping with this pain, I shifted my work schedule. I began to sleep later into the mornings and stay up late at night. I indulged in the use of marijuana, ate poorly, stopped exercising and became introspective. Soon, I became depressed. The 1973 oil embargo did not help: lights in the N.Y.C. skies were dimmed, apartments were not heated adequately, news about the Yom Kippur War was painful, all of which contributed to my psychological demise.

I believe this first Depression, along with its precipitating factors, set the stage for my first attack of Bipolarity.The excessive use of marijuana (and some opiated hashish) three to four times daily over a period of three to four weeks was undoubtedly another significant trigger. Please note that I have not consumed any marijuana for the last 40 years; I learned the hard way!

After the dark Fall and Winter months of 1973/74 came the Spring of 1974 with its lengthening daylight hours, increased luminosity and a perceived sense of well-being that contrasted sharply with the depressed state I had been experiencing. I regained interest in my research but my relationship. was still causing me emotional pain.

At one point, I had been working very intently on a theoretical cancer-initiating mechanism for several days without drink or food. I hadn't left my dormitory room for over seventy two hours when I experienced a sudden flash of insight. My recollection of that moment in 1974 is now somewhat fragmentary. I do remember having conceptualized a general method for cancer management and treatment. The concept I discovered was the result of an amalgamation of several theories, both old and new. The joy and surprise of a perceived success in my quest to find a "cure for cancer" was too much for my weakened brain and body – this is where I lost it, I simply lost contact with reality. The concept I "developed" was based on the principle of Systemic Equilibrium and 36 years later is proving to have validity and the approaches advocated in the General Theory of cancer Management are being used in the majority of cancer treatment centers around the world. Then, I recall extending this principle of Systemic Equilibrium to economic considerations, to geopolitical considerations then to demographic considerations.

Now, with the benefit of hindsight, I know with certainty that this is the exact point where my first attack of Manic-Depressive Illness began. I remember that Dr. John Zabriskie, M.D., Ph.D., who was my advisor at the time in the Biochemistry Department at Rockefeller University, took me to the Payne-Whitney Psychiatric Clinic. At the time, I was so manic that I told him he was a humanist of the heart. Dr. Zabriskie is famous for his work on Rheumatic Heart Disease and is an extremely kind man. All I can recall after that is finding me recovering in the Payne-Whitney Clinic of New York Hospital.

At the Payne-Whitney Clinic, the thing I recall the clearest was a slide show of works by the great painters from all continents including the European Impressionists. My mania-induced euphoria left me virtually ecstatic when exposed to so much harmonious beauty. During my stay, I participated in Group as well as Individual Therapy sessions. I kept repeating over and over to whoever wanted or did not want to hear that I had discovered a "cure for Cancer" and that my father was authoritarian.

My father is definitly and has always been authoritarian. However, it remained to be established whether or not the method of incremental increases of anti-cancer therapeutic doses of Chemotherapy, Radiation Therapy, Hormonal Therapy in order to gradually restore the Systemic Equilibrium without upsetting the proper functioning of the patient's body had valid practical and therapeutic value.

This notion of Systemic Equilibrium was accompanied by the following defining methodology. I thought it important to confront the noxious element (the Cancer) with Chemo, Radio, Hormonal and Immunotherapy in increasing doses at the same time as one increases the health of other party, i.e. the body. The Immune System has to be boosted in parallel with the patient's general well-being. This would comprise vitamins and minerals to be administered if deficiencies are detected and physical exercise to increase vigour and well-being. The idea is to decrease the presence, the effect and the spread of the cancer and at the same time to stimulate the body to fight back against the cancer. In this way, homeostatic equilibrium can be restored.

CHAPTER XIII
MRS. GLORIA THOMAS (1971-2008)

As I had to pay my own living expenses during my first two years at the Sloan-Kettering Institute, I took a summer job as a "mouse room" technician: breeding, crossing, weaning, and numbering mice. We constructed very valuable strains of mice which are extremely useful for genetic and immunogenetic studies. Also, I had to give my blood every 3-4 weeks ($20/pint) in order to supplement my income.

I remember when I first walked into the mouse colony room where Gloria stood like the Queen of Mice. She smiled at me and I smiled back - we knew we hit it off. Full of comedy, Gloria has been my boss, my personal advisor, friend, confidante, second mother and second sister as well as my psychological nurse during hard times. The mouse colony she single-handedly built from scratch is world famous in scientific circles.

It is ironic that before I met my former girlfriend, I was a proponent of Free Love. My routine was to meet a young lady at lunch in the cafeteria, usually a member of the hospital or university staff or a student, and invite her for 4 o'clock tea with Gloria at the mouse colony.

I had brought ample reserves of green Chinese Tea with me from Montréal and we spiked the tea with orange blossoms and sometime fresh mint leaves. After an hour or so, Gloria quietly gave me her gave her verdict as to whether the woman was worthy of further attention. We derived a great deal of pleasure from these tea parties and we still have fond memories of them. However, over one hundred young ladies were "convinced of my good intentions" by this ruse. Some called it free love but, in retrospect, it was promiscuity in full bloom.

When E.C. entered my life, she was always trouble –right from the start. Gloria consoled me, soothed my anger and frustration, and applied a balm on my heart, soul and mind. She also enlisted her three daughters, her son and her husband, all of whom welcomed me in their home in the Bronx with warmth and compassion,

This gave me courage to continue. Gloria and Dudley even made me the godfather of their only son Edward.

In short, they gave me the home in the Bronx that I did not have in Manhattan. During depressive periods, hospitalization and recovery periods, she was my only link to warmth and kindness. I have always felt her love and concern for me, both then and now, and I always will,

We have kept in touch regularly over the years. Gloria and my Godson Edward, took the Greyhound bus in the middle of winter, when the wind-chill factor was -47°C, to attend my wedding ceremony and reception, on January 4th, 1981. In times of crisis, our monthly phone conversations rapidly turned into a daily long distance lifeline between Montréal and the Bronx.

Around 1973, despite Gloria's outstanding performance and achievement in making the mouse colony what it had become, she was laid off. The repercussions were predictably catastrophic for me because her new job took her far north of Manhattan. She was no longer readily there for me in person. I felt abandoned and without support, except on weekends when I took the subway to her home in the Bronx.

Gloria was born in Kingston, Jamaica. She was a very independent child and accentuated her autonomy by going to the West Wood High School Boarding School in Trelawney where she performed very well scholastically. In 1953, she joined her parents in the United States of America and, in 1958, undertook a three year Nursing (R.N.) Programme at Beth Israel Hospital. Then she went to Hunter College for a B.A. in Psychology and, in 1960 while she was still at Hunter College, she worked at New York University as a Research Associate in Cancer Research and Immunology. In 1966, after a joint project between NYU and Sloan-Kettering, she moved to the Sloan-Kettering Institute where she became the Queen of Mice.

Now, she is retired and, despite chronic health problems, is active in Democratic Party Campaigns, in the Police Briefing Council and as a Community Liaison for the Clergy Coalition. In other words, she is a dedicated "shit disturber" and Community Activist. I love her and she is worthy of admiration for her attachment to human values, her feeling for the people of her country as well as to the people on the planet, her love for life and for God.

Coming back to my situation in 1973, when E.C. and I were battling it out, Gloria's departure from the Manhattan job could not have come at a less opportune time. She was a Trained Nurse, and was a friend as a bonus, what more did I need? I believe in divine providence - sometimes it occurs in an obvious form, sometimes it is apparent only in retrospect and sometimes it is entirely unbeknownst to us. Gloria's academic and medical training was so suited to my needs during those hard times that I believe the spirit caused us to meet and become friends in 1971: Gloria would be there later on to support me. In any case, she has been and still is a God send!

A friend is one to whom one can pour all the contents of one's heart, chaff and grain alike, knowing that the gentlest of hands will take it, sift it, keep what is worth keeping and, with the breath of loving kindness, gently blow the rest away.—Arabian Proverb

CHAPTER XIV

MY INCOMPLETE
DOCTORATE (1970-1975/77)

After a relatively good undergraduate performance, my first year at the Sloan-Kettering / Cornell in Manhattan was very successful (top grades in Medical and Graduate schools). I was offered a transfer from the Ph.D programme to an M.D. / Ph.D. programme and I declined this offer made by the late Dean Julian Rachele, Ph.D. Dr. Rachele was a good man. He was very intelligent, efficient, calm and well organized. When my sponsorship situation and financial (stipend) situation was worsening, he said to me several times: "If they are not treating you well over there [in the Sloan-Kettering Division], we would be happy to have you at the Medical College Division of the Graduate School of Medical Sciences (Cornell University)."

Having been born in May under the astrological sign of Taurus and in the Chinese year of the Ox as well, I am doubly stubborn: I declined every single one of Dr. Rachele's offers to transfer to the medical college. I wanted to stick it out, hoping for an improvement. I was a young man of 21 years and I thought that I would conquer them with my smarts and my charm. I do not regret having done that, as my research/medical studies would have been disrupted anyway by my first episode and subsequent hospitalizations.

I had three Ph.D. Programme sponsors. Two were brilliant but not very personable. The third, Dr. Norbert I. Swislocky, a Biochemist was an outstanding scientist who was helpful and kind to me, and was a friend. Another brilliant scientist who was my friend at Sloan-Kettering and had a tremendous impact on my scientific training was the late Dr. Aaron Bendich, Ph.D. Dr. Bendich was the first one to isolate DNA from human sperm and focused his research towards the fate of residual sperm after ejaculation. He grew different cell types (mouse, hamster, guinea pig and human) in vitro, added sperm and then used different techniques to monitor the ingestion of the spermatozoid by the cells into the cytoplasm, then into the nucleus and finally incorporation into chromosomal material.

Dr. Bendich and I spent countless hours discussing his scientific projects, my own projects and science in general. At one point, he offered me co-authorship of an article in <u>Nature New Biology</u>, a prestigious journal, because of the many exchanges we had had on the subject. I had also trained a couple of his technicians in the techniques of collecting mouse sperm from the vas deferens and the epidydimus under sterile conditions. I was young, un- opportunistic and excessively humble and so I declined the honor of co-authorship.

Don't be humble; you're not that great. - Golda Meir

An amusing end to this story is that in the acknowledgment section of that scientific article, Dr. Bendich expressed gratitude for my instructions on collecting sperm without reference to the species (mouse). A medical student, famous for his pranks, cut out the acknowledgement which bore my name from the article in the journal and posted it between the two elevators in the dormitory.. Medical student mentality being what it is, I found myself on the receiving end of a lot of ribbing and descriptive gestures until I realized what was happening and tore off the piece of paper!

Coming out of the Payne-Withney Clinic, I was refreshed and undertook a project to summarize some of my research work and present a Master of Science thesis. In the middle of my thesis defense presentation, Dr. Ellen Borenfreud, Ph.D. pronounced: "It's a pity; this work represents three fourths of a PhD". I had quite a lot more data in my possession and I certainly was not communicating with anyone about my "General Theory of cancer Management". In fact, from 1974 until November19, 2000, it was almost entirely repressed in my brain due to the circumstantial pain, depression, and self-imposed starvation caused by Bipolarity.

I obtained my Master of Science Degree and, since I was feeling very good, I decided to pursue my doctoral research work at the Rockefeller University as a guest student of Dr. John Zabriskie, M.D.,

PhD. while also holding down a part-time job as a technician for a clinical Pathology lab at New York Hospital.

However, the terrible jaws of depression and its anxiety and anguish overtook me in the fall and winter of 1974/1975. In the Spring of 1975, my faithful and dearest friend, Serge Segal, brought me with my books and belongings back to Montréal.

I lived at my parents' home until September 1977. Although I had a few odd jobs, I was constantly depressed with no desire to get up from the TV, wash myself or eat. In September 1977, feeling better, I returned to Cornell University to complete my PhD. However, after three months, depression set in again and again my friend Serge Segal came to New York to bring me back to Montréal. Between 1977 and 1979, there was more TV watching, depression, armchair lassitude and lack of grooming.

In great attempts it is glorious even to fail – Vince Lombardi.

CHAPTER XV

SPECIAL PSYCHIATRIC PROFESSIONALS (1973-2014+)

At Payne-Witney Clinic, I was so oblivious to my surroundings that I do not remember anything concerning the staff. From 1975 to 1979, I was treated at the Psychiatric Institute of the Jewish General Hospital and being in a dormant state, I remember only that the treatment included a lot of Psychotherapy. In 1979, due to an overload at the Jewish General Hospital emergency room, the ambulance took me to St. Mary's Hospital. The care I received there was more personalized than other facilities with more emphasis on pharmacotherapy.

At St. Mary's, I encountered many dedicated medical professionals, most notably Dr Ruiz-Navarro, Dr Kusalic, Dr. Pierre Louis, Dr Thomas Brown, and Dr. Pascal Zuardi. The latter two physicians deserve special mention for their extensive knowledge of psychiatry and their innate immense desire to heal or at least alleviate suffering. I was so moved by my contact with these doctors that I gave each of them one of my paintings as a token of my appreciation and gratitude.

Another remarkable person was Miss Buggy, a psychiatric nurse at the St. Mary's Day Center. She was the dynamo of the whole programme (1981). On our weekly outings, she very often made the entire contingent of Day Center patients walk several miles from the hospital (Côte des Neiges Ave.) to Old Montréal and back. Some parts were uphill (through Mount Royal Park) and she would encourage everyone, spurring us on to persevere – everyone was in awe of her. She said two things during group therapy that have stuck with me to this day:

Everyone, psychiatric patient or not, is responsible for his or her words and for his or her actions.

Psychiatric patients, outside the hospital, should try to avoid interacting with other psychiatric patients.

God Bless you Miss Buggy.

"There is no psychiatrist in the world like a puppy licking your face"—Ben Williams.

"Of all the medical specialties, I contend, psychiatry has the most pervasive relationship to culture. Psychiatry... is a window on a culture's source of distress and on the human consequences of such distress." – Arthur Kleinman. *Rethinking Psychiatry: From Cultural category to personal experience.*

CHAPTER XVI

MY MARRIED LIFE AND BIPOLARITY (1980-2002)

Keep your eyes open before marriage and half-shut afterwards.
—Ben Franklin

On September 8, 1979, I met Emma (not her real name), my wife to be. After an accelerated courtship, we were engaged in February of 1980 and married civilly in 1980. The religious ceremony was held on January 4, 1981 with guests from four continents present and the reception at the Ritz Carlton in Montréal. Dr. Richard Middleton, my former McGill U. advisor, referred to it as the 'Wedding of Stars'. My niece Elise recited poems on love and marriage from The Prophet by Khalil Gibran; after weeks of instruction, several pairs of young children, danced to Srauss waltzes and I composed a musical piece especially for the occasion entitled "For Emma," which I performed on a Steinway grand piano. On a comical note, I introduced the musical piece by saying "Bethoveen composed Für Elise, this is Für Emma", a statement to which the audience cracked up laughing at, as I pretended to compare myself to the great composer.

We had four children together, two boys and two girls. All four are smart and academically successful. I was able to convey to them a taste for art (all four paint), a taste for music (all play the piano well), and a respect for human life (three of them so far have been trained and have worked as lifeguards).

I love them all and did the best I could to help raise and guide them.. I made mistakes with my two sons: the first, I considered and treated as a friend and the second I overprotected. I had the time of my life with my daughters – I think I have yet to refuse them a reasonable request. All four of my have given me many reasons to be proud of them and of myself for having contributed to their biological and spiritual fertilization and their upbringing.

Joys are vitamins of the soul. – The Talmud

I was absent quite a lot from the home due to my travels across Canada and the United States of America for work and also due to frequent separations (9 major ones). This had two consequences: Firstly, Emma had to be both a father and a mother when I was away. Second, Emma had to become severe and rigorous since, with me absent, someone had to display the authority in the home. Also, after my first three episodes, I lost all my personal vigour, physical and mental, and thus was unable to fulfill my role as father figure. This created problems. In all honesty, the above- described situations made it necessary for Emma to change. From a sweet, innocent, loving, kind and adorable 22 year old young lady I married, she gradually became a strong, resilient, hardened and yet still loving Mater Famillias.

Both Emma and I have given the children a lot of love in our own ways. Emma provided educational values, discipline and rigour. I tried to give them overtly expressed love, kindness, tenderness and to guide them in such a way as to protect them from potential dangers (I am extremely safety minded).

In order to understand the effects of Manic-Depressive Illness on our marriage, it is important to start with the knowledge that, at the time of my first attack in 1974, the professionals at the Payne-Whitney Clinic referred to my crisis as an Acute Schizoid Episode. It is only in 1981 at St. Mary's Hospital, in Montréal, seven years later, during my third episode, that I was diagnosed with Manic-Depressive Illness. By that time, Emma and I were both civilly (16/06/80) and religiously (4/01/81) married. During 1980 and 1981, Emma knew that something was wrong with me psychologically and emotionally but did not know what it was - and neither did I.

Apparently, however, the shape and colour of my eyes gave Emma an overwhelming desire to cuddle with me as the feelings of nostalgia and sadness emanating from my eyes called upon her combative nature to get me out of my parents' armchair and away from the T.V. The above sentence is in Emma's own words (slightly embellished by me!). Basically, I was irresistible and she fell madly in love with me and as you know, love conquers all and everything! Kidding aside, after a year-long honeymoon period, the impact of my Bipolarity condition began to make itself felt. Both Emma and I became like watchdogs looking for the slightest indication that I was getting euphoric or depressed. This caused a lot of strain in the everyday aspect of our married life but we got used to it. It became an acceptable and necessary fact of life.

I am deeply grateful to Emma for being diligent, patient and helpful by being my manic and depressive symptomatic mirror – a duty she has performed on top of her normal parental, spousal, culinary, housekeeping, shopping, laundry (for six persons) and teaching full time in an elementary school. She accepted this mirroring role from 1981 to 2002 – twenty three years of devotion to me for a condition that was not part of the marriage deal.

What was perhaps most challenging to our relationship, however, was the irritability that sometimes accompanies Hypomania and Depression. In my case, it causes me to shout and yell at the slightest annoying or unpleasant thing. I begged Emma to make temporary allowances for my vocal behaviour during my yearly periods of irritability – I asked her at least 600 times to let me bark and leave me alone, and at all cost, not to antagonize me during those moments. However, she refused and always retorted and this fuelled my irritability and anger – leading to numerous separations. I mentioned earlier that I was a Taurean, Emma was born under the signs of Leo and the Dog (Chinese Horoscope), so in some instances I was the recipient of a double dose of rage or strokes of claws, figuratively speaking and only perceived as such, of course. In order to lighten up this discourse, let me just say that I got along with my ex-mother in law better than with Emma and that I have always indulged in telling mother in law jokes, especially in my ex-mother in law's presence. I am going to take the liberty to write 3 of my favourites:

A Q: What is the difference between my mother in law and a bull dog? A: The bulldog does not wear lipstick!

B) Q: What is the difference between an accident and a catastrophe? A: An accident is when my mother in law is drowning in the lake; A catastrophe is someone trying to rescue her!

C) C): What is the definition of mixed emotions? A: It is to watch my mother in law fall off the cliff in my brand new Cadillac!

My ex-mother in law, G-d bless her and give her a long and healthy life, took all my jokes with a lot of appreciation for my humour and displayed a lot of patience and understanding for the manifestations of my Bipolarity. It is my belief, that people who are close to someone who is fragile (whether Hypomanic or not) should make allowances and leave the irritable person alone, by him or herself – in other words: let them bark! The worst thing one can do is to antagonize an irritable hypomanic person (and this is what Emma has done for 22 years) as the intensity, volume and frequency of the screams by both parties will increase to a point where children and neighbours will be disturbed.

The fact that Emma has antagonized me during my irritable periods has led me to state a few times that "our marriage has been 1 year of heaven and 22 years of hell" and I believe her unwillingness to make allowances for my irritable periods was one of the factors leading to our eventual divorce.

The other factors for the divorce, of course, were the irritability itself and what it entails, the hypomania and full-fledged mania with all the resulting disagreements and disruption of family life. This did not create an environment conducive to peaceful, ordered, calm and non-aggressive verbal communication. In other words, I was a bear!

The most difficult and most painful moment in my life was during a hostile separation with Emma in the summer of 1987. I was irritable and very depressed (without Effexor at my disposal) and I was without ready access to my children throughout the separation. For a period of one week, I experienced a psycho-somatic hallucination of three hungry rats in my belly eating away at my entrails (I actually felt the pain and wrenched and twisted on the floor at my parents'). Through Psychotherapy, I later came to understand that the three rats gnawing at me represented my three children at that time that I missed dearly during that period.

In spite of all the arguments and bickering, Emma and I loved each other passionately, leading to the birth of our children. As a matter of fact, I remember very clearly every single one of the moments during which my four children were conceived. They were wanted in advance and cherished in our minds at that moment. While the creative accomplishment was ongoing, I could perceive all around the room a lot of Sanctity (Kédousha).

The most beautiful thing we can experience is the mysterious
It is the source of all true art and science – Albert Einstein

Despite the separations and other marital conflicts, it is obvious that Emma and I did have times when we love each other with intensity but did not like aspects of each other's personality, temperament and character. We were hard- headed and, right from the beginning; there was little room for compromise.

Our marriage lasted twenty three years, until Spring 2002 when Emma could no longer endure my Bipolarity. She deliberately stopped (she stated so at that time) being my mirror, which ultimately precipitated my fourth manic episode and a subsequent seven week hospitalization. On August 4th, 2002, during my post-discharge convalescence, Emma kicked me out of the house and I went to my parents' home for the following year. Now I have my own apartment and I spend most of my time performing volunteer work, reading, piano playing, painting and writing.

"Men marry women with the hope they will never change. Women marry men with the hope they will change, Invariably they both are disappointed" – Albert Einstein.

Obviously, I am concentrating on my rehabilitation at this point with the hope, the wish, the determination, the resolve and the conviction that soon my 2002 hospitalization will be a thing of the past and that my life will be rewarding and fruitful again. Amen!

Solitude is painful when one is young, but delightful when one is more mature—Albert Einstein

CHAPTER XVII

CANADIAN LIFE TECHNOLOGIES INC. (1983-2000)

After 1977, I worked in a variety of sales jobs and quickly discovered that I had a gift for salesmanship. I am personable, friendly and eager to assist people in the selection of their purchases. I do not pressure customers and they buy in part to please me and reward me for my good manners and the attention I afford them. Whenever I sold, I made a point of not thinking about my financial rewards if the sale went through. Thinking about personal gain is perceived negatively by the customer and detracts from the main goal which is to assist the customer and close the sale.

After Emma and I got married in 1980, I realized that a vast amount of scientific knowledge lay unused in my brain. At the same time, I also knew that I had a definite knack for sales. Why not combine the two? What I needed was a job as a salesman in a scientific environment.

In 1982, Emma found an ad in a newspaper for a salesperson for Molecular Biology products. I got the job with a company called Canadian Life Technologies, Inc. (C.L.T.I.) and immediately tripled my salary. My immediate supervisor, Mr. Ed McMahon, National Sales Manager, a tremendously kind and humorous man, quickly realized that my extensive scientific background and my budding talent in sales were going to be assets to the company and that my Bipolarity would be somewhat of a drawback.

At this point, I would like to state that when hiring and employing someone who has a Mental Illness, most notably someone who has Bipolarity, employers should take the very good with the not so good. I say very good because people with Bipolarity are unusually intelligent, creative, provide new ideas and improvements, are very industrious and productive. So when an individual with Bipolarity falters due to Depression or Mania, employers need to be understanding and patient.

My C.L.T.I. employers were very patients with regards to my medical condition and it paid off. I was Top Salesperson in Canada in 1984, 1985, 1987, 1989, 1990, 1991 and in 1993. Other years, I was not far behind the lead. It was a fun game for me. Mr Ed McMahon once wrote to me "Alain, when you are enthusiastic, you are possibly the best Sales Representative in North-America".

I remember having supper with Ed in 1984 during which he asked me whether I would prefer a plaque or money as award for making Top Salesperson in Canada. I became silent for about 45 seconds, thinking that a monetary reward as a precedent would spark competition within the sales force and damage communication during sales meetings about scientific information, exchanging leads and so on. I chose the trophy. It wasn't worth the extra couple of thousand dollars a year if it meant the atmosphere of the company and spirit of the sales force would be adversely affected. As a result of this decision, the Canadian Branch became the jewel of Life Technologies Inc. among 87 countries and famous for the collaboration and cooperation between the members of its Sales Force and the Marketing Department.

From 1998 to 2000, I lost motivation for my job at C.L.T.I. due to health, financial and marital considerations. The National Sales Manager in 2000 (J.G.) was very kind, and over ten months made me understand that the company had to lay me off. Then J.G. offered me a generous package deal which I accepted in October 2000 at which point I left C.L.T.I.

During the eighteen years I was employed at C.L.T.I., I developed excellent friendships with wonderful individuals. In fact, they became my extended family. I have kept in touch with some of them and I must mention the names of a few exceptional friends: Serge Martin, David Troock, Bob Davidson, Bill Bogle, Bob McKend, Ed McMahon and the delightful, brilliant and compassionate Monette Greenway (V.P., Europe), as they have afforded me extensive and selfless support during the frequent and difficult times and states I went through while I was working with them or in a social setting.

My best friend is the one who brings out the best in me.
—Henry Ford

One of the aforementioned friends, Bob Davidson, paid tribute to our proverbial friendship by giving my name (Alain) to his newborn daughter Alana in 1993. Obviously, I am feeling tremendously honoured by this gesture.

Special mention and thanks to the McGill Cancer Centre Staff, in Montréal, to whom I presented L.T.I. products for over 17 years. Indeed, due to my interest (obsession) in Cancer Research, they welcomed me as an equal and as one of their own.

Teamwork is the fuel that allows common people to attain uncommon results—Anonymous.

CHAPTER XVIII
MY FATHER (1919-2014+)

My father Marc is very educated, intelligent, kind and devoted to his family and friends. He lost his mother when he was seven and was raised by his older brother, the late Joseph Amzallag in a family of 13 children. He was educated at the Lycée Lyautey, a French Cultural Mission, during the protectorate of Morocco, until the French government of Vichy expelled him in mid-year because he was Jewish. Following the arrival of U.S. naval forces in Casablanca in 1943, he found employment with the American Red Cross, where he worked for three years. Then, he worked twelve years for the U.S. Air force at the Nouasseur Air Force base, quickly rising to the rank of civilian major. His duties as Chief of Civilian Personnel involved the redirecting and optimization of performance and satisfaction for approximately 6000 employees. Then, he entered a business partnership with his cousin and sold thread, wool and cotton wholesale for four years.

In 1965, the whole family immigrated to Montréal and my mother found employment as an assistant to a Department Director at the Université de Montréal. My father, after trying several venues, taught French in an English High School for 17 years. While he was teaching, he studied at night and obtained a Masters of Arts in French Literature from McGill University, followed by a B.A. in Translation from Université de Montréal.

I have never seen a person read so much for so long, so frequently, with such a diverse range of reading material and with so much enjoyment. He will turn 95 in November, 2014 – God bless him – and I believe he is a multidisciplinary scholar or at least a secular learned man. His father, the late Rabbi Moshé Amzallag was a graduate of the Marrakech Hebraic University and spent the last 30 years (he passed away at 96) of his life writing commentaries of the Kabala in Aramaic. He was offered the position of Chief Judge of the rabbinical tribunal of Casablanca. He declined, stating that the position would imply too many possibilities for human error and hence too many possibilities for deviating from the will of God.

Due to my extreme sensitivity and the fact that my father was motherless from the age of seven, I perceived my father as authoritarian, harsh, severe, somewhat abrupt and unfair well into my adulthood up until I reached the age of 40. After living with him and my mother from August 2002 to July 2003, I have come to appreciate his devotion to his children, his intense love for his wife, his willingness to help others, even strangers. He's a frugal person and yet very generous. He never let me down!

In 1974, (and in 1973 as well, when I was depressed) during my hospitalization in New York City, after a five day week of teaching he took the Greyhound bus from Montréal to visit me during the weekends. He did this for several months including during my convalescence. My father drove down with my friend Serge Segal who lived in Montreal.

There were nine separations between Emma and myself during the 23 years of marriage. I spent these separations, sometimes up to a year in duration, at my parents' home. My father and my mother – God bless them – managed my resentment toward Emma and toward life very expertly and adroitly, appeasing me at times, as I was in a hypomanic and fragile state. They never let me down.

"We are Taught you must blame your father, your sisters, your brothers, the school, the teachers – but never blame yourself. It's never your fault. But it's always your fault, because if you wanted to change you're the one who has to change."— Katharine Hepburn. *(Me: Stories of My Life).*

CHAPTER XIX

ODE TO MY MOM

דײסב

Ode to my Mom

Born in Casablanca, my mother was a person, whose main intent and purpose in life was to express her joyful kindness to people surrounding her, making them happy in the process. My Mom's predestined name is Frê'ha, a Judeo-Arabic word meaning "Joy". As far back as I can remember, she applied this joy to uplift everyone around her. All my life, she tackled my self esteem problems by encouraging me skillfully and to the hilt.

In 1974, I had my first manic episode while pursuing my graduate studies in New York City and following hospitalization, my health was in shambles. She welcomed me back in her home in Montreal and almost single handedly nursed me back to sanity and well being. She blew a wind of hope that disintegrated my feelings of helplessness. The courage that inspired me led me to start my own family. This tender loving care she provided for over a year, is what almost every mother would do for her child. However, my Mom was a support for me throughout the thirty years of my illness along with the twelve years of her own struggle with a lethal form of breast cancer. What was remarkable about my mom was so that despite the excruciating pain she was enduring, she exercised incredible restraint when I was around so that I would be spared being a witness to her own pain. This was heroic on her part, as her exuding internal fortitude was contagious and did wonders during my faltering moments. Indeed, being afflicted with Bipolar Affective Disorder, Type I, I am extremely sensitive and emotional. During twelve years she hid her pain, but at what cost…

My Mom knew what I wanted to hear, which she did not always tell me; she also knew what I needed to hear, which she delivered readily, providing me with an essential sense of identity and importance in this world. The love in her eyes spread through my chest, my soul, my heart and my mind. Only Mom could make me feel that way, in an instant! As you know, megalomania is a phenomenon often associated with Bipolar Disorder, and this scourge eventually led to my personal bankruptcy.

> *Beware of small expenses. A small leak will sink a great ship.*
> –Ben Franklin

Although my salary was in the six figures, I was always short of cash. My Mom scolded me for spending too much money, but occasionally gave me a $20 bill despite the fact she was living on a pension. This is one of the many examples of the self abnegation she practiced routinely. While her cancer was spreading, she continued to exercise her hospitality duties, as usual. She would host 12 to 15 guest dinners on Jewish holidays such as Passover and Rosh Hashanah. My own family was always invited and very few people were aware of her medical condition because she was so welcoming and cheerful. As a matter of fact, she instructed her immediate family not to divulge her illness to anyone. She wanted to live her life to the fullest until very close to the end. In the face of such unshaken resolve, courage and indomitable morale, my own seasonal anguishes and anxieties quickly dissipated.

When I was irritable, I took refuge at my Mom's home, where I knew I would not be antagonized. She left me alone, and waited until I requested attention. She would then softly allay my fears and calm down my inner demons with her soothing voice. Some may call it babying or excessive tender loving care, but my Mom knew instinctively that the way she acted was in fact "What the doctor ordered". Before cancer struck, Mom, she handled my depressions over the phone, six to eight times a day. Again, with her loving and soothing voice, she would welcome me in her home in the middle of the afternoon for a 2-hour nap. She recognized the importance of sleep in depressed states. My Mom protected my sleep like a watchdog, thus avoiding an upsurge of irritability.

By far, my Mom was the most inspirational figure in my life. She displayed strength, resilience, courage and hope for herself and for her loved ones. She also taught me that in managing my condition I have to make adjustments and personal concessions in order to limit, and build resistance, to internal and external stress.

<u>Mom was Tall</u>   <u>My Mom stood Tall</u>   <u>My Mom stands Tall</u>
<u>in my heart</u>.

<u>I love you Mom</u>   <u>I miss you Mom</u>

CHAPTER XX
A FEW CLOSING REMARKS

I would like to conclude this guide with a note of optimism. There are several negative aspects to Bipolarity such as manic episodes, depression, and irritability as well as the effects of these symptoms on employment status and family life. On the other hand, Bipolarity confers a very high degree of intellectual capacity and ability to think conceptually with ease and a good measure of creativity that can be expressed in Art, Music, Business, Politics, as well as several other endeavours.

Overall, I believe that my life up to now has been good. I thank the Lord for my life before and after the onset of my illness and I am thoroughly embracing, with eager expectations, the prospect of a rewarding and fruitful remainder of my life.

God Bless you all!
Alain Abraham Amzallag, Ph.D. (ABD).
Montreal, Canada

"May the second half of your life be better than your first"
—Arabian Blessing.

ACKNOWLEDGEMENTS

- I am deeply grateful to Mrs. Gloria Alexander for her love and support over the course of the 37 years during which we have been friends.

- I have been privileged to have Mr. Serge Segal as a scouting brother, legal advisor and extremely dependable friend for over
47 years. Serge has very high standards of personal integrity and professionalism and I respect him greatly.

- I have also been blessed to know and interact with Ms. Sarita Benchimol, Associate to the Director at the McGill Cancer Centre, as she kept me abreast of cancer research development for several years and also provided me with support during my depressive and manic ordeals. She is kind, focused and energetic i.e. "The Dynamo".

-I am grateful to Dr LeRoy Spaniol, of the faculty of the Rehabilitation Counseling Program in the Sargent College of Health and Rehabilitation Sciences at Boston University, Boston, Massachusetts for reviewing the chapter on Rehabilitation and for providing judicious advice.

I would like to thank the team of Jean Coutu pharmacists who have provided me for many years with important information concerning the side effects of the many medications that are prescribed to me. They are: Amina Mékouar, Ph.; Alina Schaidulina, Ph.; Makan Dabo, Ph.; and Hajar Ennajimi, Ph.

APPENDIX:

Theoretical and Practical Notions
in Cancer Immunotherapy

WRITTEN NOVEMBER 20th, 2000 (1974)

In the early 1970's, a prevalent theory about cancer postulated that it is an imbalance of the Homeostasis of the organism. The author still believe this is largely true. Indeed, the exposure to radiation, chemical mutagens and/or oncogenic viruses will result in the accumulation of mutations in the DNA sequence (oncogenes) and neoplasia will ensue. If DNA Repair and later the Immune Surveillance mechanisms are not able to cope with these mutations past a genetically predetermined threshold, cancer will occur.

The mechanism by which the loss of contact inhibition, invasiveness and metastasia operate is at the cell surface level. Cell membrane surface components mediate morphogenetic movement in tissues of healthy organisms and this cell movement goes awry in cancer. In practical terms an as yet untested approach to attempt to treat cancer would be to expose cell surface tumor specific antigens from cancer cells or tissues by a variety of mechanical techniques including mincing, sonicating and/or slow and partial enzyme mediated dissociation, etc.... of the tumor cell membrane, while ensuring that the antigenic determinants such as glycoproteins arenot modified, altered or denatured. Then the emulsion (adjuvant?) would be administered to the patient and presumably the antigenic determinants in the self originating vaccine would have become immunogenic and would elicit an immune response directed towards the tumor specific antigens of the cancer cells and/or tissues. In this fashion the homeostatic equilibrium should be restored and would be concomitant with a return to health.

I also think that cancer therapy ought to be performed in small steps and incremental doses. In this fashion, treating with Chemo, Radio, Hormone and/or Immuno Therapies will not result in the additional perturbation of the already precariously affected Homeostasis.

Acknowledgments:

These notions stem from studies at McGill University (Genetics), Cornell University & Sloan-Kettering Institute (Immunogenetics) and Rockefeller University (Immunocardiology). I am deeply grateful to all my professors, physicians, advisors, friends and my family.

ABOUT THE AUTHOR

Alain was born in Casablanca. He "purports" to be the "spiritual son" of Humphrey Bogart and Ingrid Bergman. Kidding aside, in 1965 he moves to Montréal and his Scientific / Medical studies take him from McGill University through Cornell University Medical College / Sloan-Kettering Institute to Rockefeller University in N.Y.C. In 1974, Alain falls ill with an episode of Bipolar Affective Disorder and this book's intent is to convey an understanding of Bipolarity, as well as a message of hope since Bipolarity can be managed to a satisfactory extent. Back in Montréal, Alain undertakes a brilliant eighteen year career as a Senior Sales Representative with Canadian Life Technologies Inc., and he is blessed with four talented and wonderful children

To contact the author:
alainamzallag@bell.net
www.alainamzallag.com